BLACK TOFFEE in association with
HARROGATE THEATRE present:

HIDDEN

by

Laura Lindsay and Peter Carruthers

Published by Playdead Press 2013

© Laura Lindsay and Peter Carruthers 2013

Laura Lindsay and Peter Carruthers have asserted their rights under the Copyright, Design and Patents Act, 1988, to be identified as the authors of this work.

A CIP catalogue record for this book is available from the British Library.

ISBN 978-0-9576792-0-7

Caution

All rights whatsoever in this play are strictly reserved and application for performance should be sought through the authors via www.hiddenplay.co.uk/contact before rehearsals begin. No performance may be given unless a licence has been obtained.

This book is sold subject to the condition that it shall not by way of trade or otherwise be lent, resold, hired out or otherwise circulated without the publisher's prior consent in any form of binding or cover other than that in which it is published and without a similar condition including this condition being imposed on the subsequent purchaser.

Printed by BPUK

Playdead Press
www.playdeadpress.com

CAST:

Claire / Nina / Cara	**Laura Lindsay**
Colin / Gareth / James	**Peter Carruthers**

CREATIVE TEAM AND CREW:

Writers	**Laura Lindsay**
	Peter Carruthers
Dramaturg/Original Director	**Martin Jameson**
Edinburgh Fringe/Tour Director	**Helen Parry**
Set Designer	**Alex Swarbrick**
Original Set Design	**Martin Jameson**
	Laura Lindsay
Lighting Design/Stage Manager	**Mark Creamer**
Sound Design	**Owen Rafferty**
Composer	**Harri Chambers**
Movement Consultants	**Neil Bettles**
	Ceris Faulkner
Photography	**Kate Eden**
Trailer	**Lucy Lincoln**
	Amy McIntyre
	Owen Rafferty
Production Manager	**Laura Lindsay**
Co-Producer	**Kevin Jamieson**
Executive Producer	**Jim McDonnell**

With special thanks to:

Underbelly for staging Hidden as part of The Edinburgh Festival Fringe 2013, Manchester Library Theatre and The Lowry for staging Hidden at Re:play Festival 2013 and Harrogate Theatre for their invaluable support and advice.

WRITERS AND CAST
Claire / Nina / Cara // **Laura Lindsay**

Hidden is Laura's writing debut. Since graduating from The Arden School of Theatre in 2010, Laura's theatre credits include: Felicity in *You Once Said Yes*, Jenna in *Above and Beyond* (both with Look Left Look Right), Gamma in *Borderline Vultures* (The Lowry), Nurse Bragg in *The Interpreter* (24:7 Theatre Festival), Casey in *All Because of Molly* (Lowry Studio and NW tour), Zoe in *The Enemy Within* (RNCM) and Isabella in *Measure for Measure*. Laura's screen credits include *Prisoners' Wives* (BBC 1), Emmerdale (ITV 1) and several short films. Radio credits include: *China Girl* (BBC Radio 4) and *Rooftop Romeo* (BBC Radio 3). Laura is represented by Northern Lights Management. **Spotlight VIEW PIN: 3812-7863-7058**

Colin / Gareth / James // **Peter Carruthers**

Hidden is also Peter's writing debut. Since writing *Hidden* he has gone on to write *Fallout* (WINNER: Best Short Film at the GI Film Festival 2013 in Washington DC) and *Never Forget* (selected from almost 2,000 entries to be part of a feature length collection of 50 short films called *50 Kisses* which is set for global distribution later in 2013). Peter graduated from The Arden School of Theatre in 2009. Theatre credits since graduating include: Boyfriend Jack in *Beat Surrender* (RNCM and Re:play 2011), Carl in *The Enemy Within* (RNCM), George in *Under My Skin* (regional tour), Dave in *Plus One..?* (Lowry Studio), Tony in *Abigail's Party* (Salford Arts Theatre) and Man in *More Light* (Nexus Arts Café and Bakewell Arts Festival). Peter's film credits include: *Will Power* (2012) and several short films. Peter is currently seeking representation. **Spotlight VIEW PIN: 5413-6723-1805**

PRODUCERS

Laura and Peter formed Black Toffee in 2011, with the aim of producing new, high quality theatre and film which reflect modern society and challenge perspectives. They met during training at The Arden School of Theatre where they discovered a mutual love of new writing, an interest in human psychology and a shared dark sense of humour. In addition to *Hidden*, Black Toffee has also produced Peter's two short films *Fallout* and *Never Forget*. The company is in pre-production for another short film, *Civvy Street*, commissioned by the NHS. After the Edinburgh Festival Fringe, Black Toffee is touring *Hidden* in association with Harrogate Theatre. Any theatres interested in programming as part of the tour are invited to contact us via our website: **www.hiddenplay.co.uk/contact**

Harrogate Theatre's **Associate Company Scheme** supports, mentors, champions and develops artists and performers of the future by giving them access to artistic and business support, professional development and rehearsal space, as well as opportunities to showcase their work. Harrogate Theatre wholeheartedly believes that's how small companies can afford to make great theatre with big ideas and grow to be the big hitters of tomorrow. We're happy to help with whatever they need to create, survive and thrive.

ORIGINAL DIRECTOR // **Martin Jameson**

Martin is a writer, director and producer. He has enjoyed a varied career in theatre, TV and radio. He was associate director at Nottingham Playhouse, and directed for many companies nationwide including The Young Vic and West Yorkshire Playhouse. Martin has also enjoyed an extensive writing career. BAFTA nominated for his work on *Children's Ward*, he was also on the team the year that *Emmerdale* received the BAFTA gong. He has worked extensively for *Holby*, *Casualty*, *The Bill* and *EastEnders*. Martin's great passion is radio drama and he has penned more plays for the medium than he can count, most recently the classic series *Angel Pavement* (starring Marcus Brigstocke).

EDINBURGH FESTIVAL FRINGE and TOUR DIRECTOR // **Helen Parry**

Helen originally trained as an actor at what was Manchester Polytechnic (now Manchester Metropolitan University) and has had a diverse career in acting, directing and teaching. She was an acting tutor at The Arden School of Theatre before recently returning to freelance directing. Her directing work includes productions in Germany, Switzerland and the USA where she also participated in a teaching exchange programme in Florida. In the UK, her productions have been staged locally at The Library Theatre, Contact Theatre, The Royal Exchange Studio and The Green Room. Some of this work went on to tour nationally and included venues such as the ICA and the Cochrane Theatre, London, Birmingham Rep Studio and Leicester Haymarket Studio.

SET DESIGN // **Alex Swarbrick**
Alexander graduated from the Cambridge School of Art, with a BA in Film and Theatre Design. He has designed productions for Thunder Road, Harrogate and Ripon Youth Theatre and has constructed sets for Sheffield Crucible, York Theatre Royal and Hull Truck Theatre. Previous designs include *The Count of Monte Cristo* (Thunder Road), *Awkward/Burn* (Harrogate Theatre Youth Club) and *Boiling Frog* (Humruddy Productions).

LIGHTING DESIGN and
STAGE MANAGER // **Mark Creamer**
Mark has taken productions to The Lowry, Cornerstone Theatre, Liverpool Lantern and Studio Salford. He has also toured to the Edinburgh Fringe Festival, Preston Tringe and Buxton Festival. He is the Technical Manager for 24:7 Theatre Festival, having worked for them for the past nine years. He has also worked as a Venue Technician for Pleasance Theatre Edinburgh. He is currently employed as a Production Technician at University of Salford which he does alongside being the Technical Manager for HOPE Theatre Company.

SOUND DESIGN // **Owen Rafferty**
Owen graduated in 2010 with a distinction in Audio Engineering from the School of Sound Recording in Manchester. He has spent the past three years dedicating himself to sound design work on the fringe theatre scene. His credits include sound design for *Dev's Army* (Not Part of Festival 2011 - winner of a "Forever Manchester" award), *Loaded* (24:7 Festival 2012) and *Lamp Oil* (The Eagle Inn, Salford). He also composed the soundtrack for *The Interpreter* (24:7 Festival 2012) and did sound and lighting design for "One Hand Clapping", an adapted work that played at the International Anthony Burgess Foundation in March 2013.
His most recent sound design projects have been *The Man Who Woke Up Dead* by Square Peg and *Away from Home* by Working Progress Theatre.

COMPOSER // **Harri Chambers**

Harri is a performer, composer and producer who has just completed his final year at Goldsmiths College in London. In addition to theatre work, he is an instrumentalist in many ensembles and bands. Harri creates his solo work under the alias 'King of Hearts'. Check him out on Soundcloud where you can hear many of the tracks featured in *Hidden*. Equipped with a miniature recording device everywhere he goes, Harri makes much of his music from the sounds of everyday life.

MOVEMENT CONSULTANT // **Neil Bettles**

Neil is co-founder and Artistic Director of ThickSkin. Directing credits for ThickSkin include: *The Static*, *Blackout*, *Overture* and *These Imagined Stories*. Co-direction for ThickSkin includes *Boy Magnet* and *White Noise*. As Associate Director / Choreographer Neil's credits include: *Blood Wedding* and *The Bacchae* for The Royal and Derngate's Festival of Chaos 2012 and *The Full Monty* for Sheffield Theatres; and as Associate Director *Beautiful Burnout* and *Lovesong* for Frantic Assembly. Other movement direction includes: *Much Ado About Wenlock* for Vamos Theatre (UK tour), *Platform* (Old Vic Tunnels), *Henry IV Part One* (Drum Theatre Plymouth), *Secret Cinema* for Frantic Assembly and *Stanley Pickle*, an animated short film by Vicky Mather for the National Film and Television School (winner of 31 awards worldwide). He is Creative Associate for Frantic Assembly's Ignition Project, co-directing numerous productions since 2008. He was also Assistant Director for Frantic Assembly's *Dirty Wonderland*. Neil is currently Video Designer for *In an Alien Landscape* for Birds of Paradise.

MOVEMENT CONSULTANT // **Ceris Faulkner**

Ceris trained at both Rambert and Royal Ballet Schools. She was a founder member of London City Ballet where she worked as a soloist and principle character dancer. She performed at the Nureyev Festival at The London Colliseum, Scottish Opera, The Royal Albert Hall, Festival Hall and The Barbican as well as on various productions for the BBC. Following her move to Manchester she became Artistic Director of Gestures Dance Company. She has choreographed for Ensemble Cymru and St Asaph International Music Festival as well as a national tour of Beatrix Potter in Welsh. She is currently part of Manchester City Art Galleries Artists in Schools project, the movement coordinator for Parry Productions and also a dance tutor at Steelworks Academy and Shockout Academy.

PHOTOGRAPHER // **Kate Eden**

Kate is a doctor with an interest in photography. She specialises in landscape photography, but she also has a flair for portraits and still life. Kate took all the production and publicity shots for *Hidden*.

PATRONS OF BLACK TOFFEE

Heartfelt thanks to the patrons of Black Toffee who have financially supported us through our Kickstarter Project. We could not have done it without your support.
Thank you.

Assembled Junk Productions
Michelle Ashton
Alex Butcher
Indira Butcher
Teri Centner
Peter and Gerry Clarke
Kathy Dodworth
Denise Hobart
Nicholas Hussey
Kevin Jamieson
Tony Kennick
William Lindsay
Peter and Marie Louch

Elaine and Graham McMillan
Winifred McDonnell
Adam Medcalf
Wynn Moran
Hekate Papardaki
Helen Parry
Gordon Richardson
Craig and Joanna Sells
Richard Taylor
Stuart Thomas
Heather and Dave Treweeke
Craig Walton

With Kind Support From:

michael pollard
photographer
manchester

tel : 0161 456 7470
email : info@michaelpollard.co.uk
website : www.michaelpollard.co.uk

Jennifer Bea

Howard Ellis

CHARACTERS:
In order of appearance

Colin
Mid 30s, Northern

Claire
33, Glaswegian

Nina
30, RP

Gareth
Early 30s, London

Cara
28, Northern

James
Mid 30s, RP

SCENE 1:   Colin: PART 1

Colin is in the audience.

You're sat in the theatre right. You're sat there watching this play and it's... ok, I mean it's not amazing, but it's, you know, keeping your attention. I don't know, maybe there's the odd laugh where there should be, and people are keeping quiet when there's a serious bit. It's definitely not shit. Oh no, it's not one of those times when you're like, 'HUFF! this is shit!' No, it's better than that, but it's not amazing.

Anyway, there's this serious bit, a love scene, the lad is declaring his love for... and he's doing alright, I mean the girl's way better, and she's got huge... stage presence, but he's giving it a good go. And you're kind of with him. But then, out of nowhere, you just get this... *urge* to shout out at the top of your voice, RAAAARRGGH or run onto the stage...

He runs on stage.

...get your arse out and jump about like a dick. Just to see what would happen.

Yeah, well that's what I'm talking about. That split second where you go a little bit mental in the head.

But you don't actually do it do you? You don't actually get up there.

No, you just do a little 'hmmhmmhmm oh what am I like!?' at yourself for thinking it, and then you get back to the play.

I get 'em all the time me, urges, like... erm...

Big high balcony on the umpteenth floor of a tower block: you're looking out across the stunning city sky line, beautiful sunset. But then you glance down, just for a second and all you wanna do is jump. And you imagine how it would feel to have the air rushing past you as you hurtle towards the tarmac. And how much it would hurt. Or would it?

Or... At work, last week. Strategy meeting: Nina's ranting on about coterminous targets, whatever the fuck they are. Cara's pretending to listen, but the only thing she's targeting is the last wagon wheel on the biscuit tray. Anyway, we're all feigning interest, Nina's using words that I can't even say, let alone fucking understand and all I want to do is put my head between her massive tits and go (*moves his head from side to side*), just to loosen her up a bit, you know?

Or after work... Piccadilly station, platform 14, teatime-ish, and there's this little kid, about 4 or 5. About this big, scruffy blonde hair, one hand in his pants, other one up his nose. His mum's miles away, texting on her Blackberry. Anyway, he manages to pull out this massive bogey, and I mean seriously impressive, like, it had a tail and everything! He was properly pleased with himself and I'm just looking at him and I'm thinking 'go on little fella, go on... eat it.'

Then this long freight train comes rumbling past, and I look back at this kid, and my head just goes 'grab, over the edge, snotty face, freight container, BOSH!' Whoohoo! Imagine that! Seriously, what the fuck!

Then I look down. (*beat*) My hand's sort of... I mean it's actually...

His hand is straining forwards, trying to reach out.

All on its own, like there's this snarling wild dog straining at a rope and I can't hold it.

Now I know you're probably thinking 'why have I brought this psycho back to my flat?' Oh, and now you're thinking whether you can make it to the door. And now you've remembered that you locked the door...

His phone starts to ring loudly – pulling him out of his trance. He quickly pulls it out of his pocket and answers it.

Hiya... Yeah, yeah course I am... ah yeh whoops! ...How about The Severed Arms? Right ok, well I'll be setting off in about 5 minutes.

...Erm, yeah a little bit I suppose, are you? ...Ha! I'm not that scary am I? Yeah, I know what you mean, but we'll just have a drink and a chat and... and see what happens yeah... ok, I'll see you in a bit... bye!

The call ends and he looks down at his phone.

See what happens.

SCENE 2:   Claire: PART 1

Claire enters with a box full of boxes of condoms and boxes of lube.

Och! God! I hate stacking shelves, it has got to be THE most borin' job in the world. I wouldnae mind, but havin' to stack boxes of condoms an' lube when I'm getting none of... 'that' mahself is just taking the piss! (*stares at the box of condoms*) "Expiry date: November 2016" Well, you've got more chance o' seein' sum action before you expire than me pal! (*beat*) Jesus Christ! I'm talking to a box a jonnies! (*listens to the box*) eh, steady on! Ah well, I'm on the tills later, at least then I get to haver chat with *people*. And haver nose at their shoppin' and make wild judgements aboot 'em. And who knows maybe Mr Right'll come up my aisle this afternoon, he he!

Interrupted by Nina asking where the pregnancy tests are:

Ooh sorry love I didnae see you there! Yeh it's doon the same aisle as the toilet roll. Eh? Clear Blue? Och y'mean the tests to see if yer up the duff? Yeh they're just there, by yer knee. Ironic that that they're next to the contraception eh?

Watches Nina as she leaves without thanking her:

No, no my pleasure! That's it on ye go, without a word of thanks.

Hey Mary! I'm dyin' fae a piss, can I go on ma break now pleaze? Daft bitch cannae hear me! I'll just sneak off, naeone'll notice.

SCENE 3: Nina

SFX: A toilet flushing.

Nina stands, pregnancy stick in hand.

Isn't something supposed to happen? (*beat – stares at the test*) Isn't something supposed to kick in – nature's instinct – some kind of... *compulsion* to procreate? Well, I'm still waiting!

I tell you something, if this is negative I'm going to... thank the Lord, Jesus, Mohammed, Vishnu, fucking... Aslan... and then pour a massive glass of Chardonnay. And book myself in to get neutered. I don't want a baby. I really, really don't want to be pregnant. Please! (*stares at stick*) I'm not ready to be a mother (*correcting herself*) I don't *want* to be a mother...

I mean, I guess I thought... maybe, someday in the far off, theoretical, hypothetical – probably won't be realised – future – but now... Oh God! We've just got new carpets!

All of my friends have got... stained carpets... or are about to. I know I'm an oddity. They've all taken to motherhood like it's their vocation, their entire reason for being. You know what I mean, they have that... superior air that people who come back from travelling have – that somehow, they are better than you, but you couldn't possibly understand why, until you join their ranks. Their ranks of... talking about potty-training, meal planning and C fucking Beebies! They've all stopped asking me 'Nina, when do you think you'll...', but I still feel their silent, supercilious... milky-titted judgement.

I'm sick of people at work cooing at babies and clucking at the mere thought of having them. Cara, for example, I doubt she's ever even had a boyfriend, but she was blabbering in the lift – in between mouthfuls of Wagon Wheel – about how she's already chosen her babies' names. Ridiculous! It's like a... virus, but somehow I'm immune.

(*looks at the pregnancy stick – it isn't ready*) Oh come on – put me out of my misery! (*beat*) Fuck what will James say? We've never really talked about kids, it's just not... come up. I guess I assumed that he feels the same... apathy I do, else he'd have started pestering me by now, wouldn't he? I mean I'm 30.

30. Biological clock: tick tock. Viable eggs: plip plop. Into the filthy omelette of the sewer. Denied the chance of life by me – the mother hen. (*beat*) In evolutionary terms the entire purpose of an individual is to... create more life. I'm going to have to do something pretty special in my own lifetime to justify my 'opt-out' policy. But I work in the civil service – what, of any significance, can I possibly do here?! My management of coterminous target pathways is the envy of the department, it's true. But I don't think it quite off-sets my... lack of contribution to the furtherment of the species.

It's not that I don't like kids... I do... they can be 'fun', but they're so demanding and exhausting. You have to pretty much give up any sense of self and be prepared to dedicate your entire time, energy and money to a screaming ball of flesh. And I don't want to do that – I like my life as it is. Just us. I don't want to have to factor anyone else into our lives. (*beat*) I mean... I'm not even sure our relationship would... (*trails off*) Do you know what? Fuck the Chardonnay! If this is negative I'm going to crack open that bottle of Chateauneuf du Pape we've been saving.

I'm not saying... I mean I do... I am good with... I like spending time with my nieces – they are very cute and I'm very good with them – even if I do say so myself. But they do get a bit pissing irritating after a couple of hours. Maybe it'd be different with my own... *our* own children. People always say that, don't they. But *how* do you know? And what do you do if it's not? I mean it's not like you can go 'ah yes hello I'd like to return this baby please, yes here's my receipt. No, no nothing wrong with it, we just got it home and realised it doesn't really suit us.'

(*looks again at the pregnancy test*) Oh shit, is that a line? Does that mean I'm pregnant? (*looks at instructions on the box*) Yes it does. (*looks back at the test*) But that's... not a line, I don't think, uh I'm not sure. I'll leave it another minute. (*beat*) Jesus this is so undignified. Pissing on a stick. Surely if I *am* pregnant the hormones will be permeating my entire body and will be present in all my... fluids so why the hell can't they invent a test for your saliva?

Pause

The thing is... if that is negative and I manage to avoid pregnancy happily ever after, will I get to 45 and regret *not* doing it? Does it make me less of a woman? Will my arms yearn and my womb ache as it shrivels into... a desolate desert where no life is possible? You know, perhaps having children is the only effective distraction from the inevitable decline towards death. (*beat*) Pffff... that's a bit morbid.

Pause

Maybe it wouldn't be so bad.

Pause

Maybe a child will... fill the void I've never... admitted is there, but it is (*trails off*)...

Here goes nothing...

SCENE 4: Gareth and Cara

Works canteen. Gareth is on his lunch. He has sausage and chips. He is sitting nervously contemplating a whole sausage on the end of his fork. He studies it. He looks around. He tries motioning it towards his open mouth, whole, lengthways. Savouring it, he delicately puts it in his mouth and gently bites a chunk off it and chews it slowly, pleasurably in his mouth, eyes closed.

Cara comes over to Gareth's table with a salad. She hovers by the empty chair.

Cara: Hiya, d'you mind if I sit here?

Gareth is absorbed in his sausage-based fantasy, but this makes him jump. He starts to choke on the sausage. He is struggling to breathe. Cara watches, unsure what to do. She then hurriedly puts her salad down, puts her arms round Gareth and performs the Heimlich manoeuvre three times. Gareth eventually coughs the sausage up onto his plate and gasps for breath.

Pause

Cara: So *can* I sit here?

Gareth: (*still out of breath*) Erm... puuuphhh... yeh sure.

Cara sits down. Silence. Gareth is regaining his breath.

Cara: You work on the third floor don't you?

Gareth: errr yeah.

Cara: I'm on the fifth floor, Nina's team. (*pause*) Y'know, the snooty one. Thinks she runs the department (*giggles awkwardly*) No, she's alright really... just passionate about targets!

Awkward pause

> And you must know Colin? Weird, starey Colin...? No he's nice really, just, you know... stares... a lot...

Awkward pause

> (*blurts*) You get in the same lift as me...

Gareth: Ah right... er cool.

Cara: Up and down, up and down (*laughs awkwardly*).

Awkward pause

> Though you won't have seen me recently cos I've not been taking the lift – I've been using the stairs. Well just today actually, but you know... you have to start somewhere! (*beat*) So I thought seeing as I'd not seen you in the lift, I'd come over and say hi now... (*pause, waves*) "Hi"

Gareth: Hi.

Cara: Sorry about making you choke.

Gareth: Nah, nah it's alright, I was just thinking about someone (*correcting himself*) something (*correcting himself again*) erm work – stuff and you made me jump. Didn't see you, y'know?

Silence

Gareth: Thanks for… well… saving my life, I suppose!

Cara: No problem – I'm first aid trained. (*beat*) I'm Cara by the way.

Gareth: Ah right hi Cara, I'm Gareth.

Cara: I know. (*hurriedly to cover up*) You know… from your ID badge

Gareth looks down. He is not wearing his ID badge.

Cara: I saw it in the lift. Yesterday. (*beat*) you're from down South aren't you?!

Gareth: …Yeah.

Silence

Gareth: Ha! Salad!

Cara: Yeh.

Gareth: What's on that then? Other than leaves?

Cara: Cottage cheese. Tomatoes. Peppers.

Gareth: You got any cucumber? I like cucumber.

Cara: (*studying the salad*) Erm no I don't think so.

Gareth: (*realising the connotation of what he's said*) I mean I don't like cucumber... *exclusively*... y'know... I... I... I... mean I like tomatoes as well. You're allowed to like both aren't you?

Cara: (*utterly bewildered*) Yes I guess so. (*beat*) I'm not keen on either to be honest. I'd much rather have... (*looking longingly at his plate*) Sausage and chips.

The half-eaten sausage is still stuck on Gareth's fork, on the edge of his plate (next to the coughed-up sausage). He picks it back up and studies it again.

Pause

Cara: Are you actually going to eat that?

Gareth: Yeh. (*beat*) I think I am actually.

Pause

Cara: (*blurting*) Gareth. Would you like to do this somewhere else. Like I don't know... not in the work's canteen. Like, eat in a room. Somewhere else. Together?

Gareth: You mean... like a date?

Cara: (*flustered*) Yeh I suppose I do.

Gareth: No!

Cara: Oh I'm sorry...

Gareth: No I'm sorry... (*struggles to remember her name*) Cara? I mean you're... y'know beautiful... I just don't think you're my... type.

He gets up to leave.

I'll leave you to your salad.

Cara sits staring at her salad. She looks over at the sausage and chips. Eventually she reaches over for the sausage and takes a big bite.

SFX: Shop announcement: over scene change

Mary: Would the owner of a Ford Transit van currently parked in a disabled bay please come to customer services. You just need to *walk* back to the entrance area. We know you can.

SCENE 5:   Claire: PART 2

(*To customer*) Y'want any help with y' packin'? Oh sorry, y've only got two items, guess you can manage then, ey? (*expecting a laugh from the customer or at least an acknowledgement – but no reaction*) Right, well that's four nine'y eight. Would y'like any cash back? Enter your pin pleaze. Thank you.

(*To audience*) I'm sick of bein' ignored and treated like some kinda subhuman piece of shite! Contrary to popular belief the supermarkit is no' a place to meet your ideal man. Huh! No sign of Mr Right todae! I've even resorted to advertisin' mahself on the inte'net tae get *any* intrest from the male species. Dating sites: I hadnae dun them before now. I was nae sure wha' tae put. I mean what can I say aboot mahself? Claire, 33, smoker, live in a coonsil flat, would like tae meet... a man... *any* man who's not as much of a dick as him! (*indicating customer*) Fuckin' arsehole in a suit. Wi' his inspirational dinner: minced meat and tatties.

I've got used to his type mind. I've worked here for two years. It's awright I suppose – regular hours, overtime if I want it: predictable. Aye, I'm part of the ubiquitous Walmart family. (*beat*) Ubiquitous. (*indicating customer*) He'd 'a' been surprised at that – me using words like ubiquitous. He'd have assumed I'm thick. Most people think that cos I work at Asda, that's all I'm capable of. But it's no'.

I mean, aye, I rarely get aw six cheeses in Trivial Pursuit and I havnae *ever* got the conundrum on Coontdoon. I cannae speak any languages, beyond ordering a pint. I havnae made any ground-breakin' scientific discoveries – aw I lear' in Science was how tae pu'a condom on a Bunsen burner – had a surprise when I saw my first penis I can tell yer.

God it's so fuckin' long since I've seen a penis, I'm afraid I'll forget what tae dae with it. Getting ahead of mahself there though. Get a date first. A *sui'able* date. And do NOT sleep w'him on the first Claire! (*beat*) I dae *really* want sex though. A bit of the dir'y stuff. I want some excitement – summat tae get mah blood pumpin'. (*beat*) Ah'm no' fussy who with t'be honest – nae boring fuckers, nae Rangers fans and nae psychos. Simple.

SCENE 6:   James

SFX: Train noise throughout

I leave my house at 7:55 every morning. I leave my house every weekday morning at exactly 7:55 because I know that after a brisk 12 minute walk, I will arrive at the station at precisely 8:07. By 8:08 I have walked down the path to the platform and by 8:09 I have crossed the bridge and arrived at 'my spot' with one minute to spare before the prompt arrival of the little three carriage 8:10 to Victoria.

Yes, like everyone else on the platform, I have my own 'spot'. Every day the same faces stand, waiting on their marks, desperately avoiding eye contact with their fellow commuters.

And that's strange isn't it? You see these people every day, sometimes for years, you sit with them, you even stand squashed against their sweaty bodies, but you never say hello, you never nod or smile, and you never ever exchange names. No, there's an unspoken understanding, the commuters code: 'I'm here to go to work, I'm going to read Lord of the Rings and you will not interact with me, ever.'

And that is why, every day, I get on the train with Gandalf and Frodo and lose myself in Middle-Earth until I reach Victoria.

Or at least, that's how it was until very recently.

About two weeks ago, I was sitting at my usual table, totally immersed in the siege of Gondor, when I noticed something. Something was touching my knee. I looked up to see a lady sitting opposite me, head back, eyes closed, pink headphones, smiling away to herself. I recognised her straight away; she was 'tallish woman with dark hair who gets on at Horwich Parkway'. I'd never been that struck by her to be honest, I always thought she was fairly plain looking, maybe a size 14, mid to late 20's, nothing special, although I always thought she had a nice coat.

It was her knee. Her knee was touching my knee, which, as all commuters know, is strictly against the rules. My instinct of course, was to subtly move my leg away, to restore the mandatory distance. But I didn't. Something inside me said 'no... she put it there, she can move it.' I wondered if it was a simple question of space. Fat Girl with Bacon Butty who gets on at Lostock had wedged herself next to her. But I stealthily checked and saw that her overhang was into the aisle rather than encroaching on Tallish Woman's space. So I waited, totally expecting her to realise what she was doing, she would move her leg, maybe apologise and that would be that. But she didn't, it stayed there and before long it wasn't just touching, it was resting!

I couldn't believe how brazen she was being. I looked at her face, trying to work out if she was asleep, I couldn't be sure, maybe she was, but then I noticed her fingers clasped together on her stomach tapping away to the beat in her headphones. She was awake alright; she knew exactly what was going on.

I sat there, hypnotised, all the way from Bolton to Salford, frozen, sensing the weight and heat of her leg against mine. I looked over at Fat Girl - bacon butty demolished - engrossed in Take a Break, completely unaware of what was going on under her table. I was trying to remember where Tallish Woman usually got off, was it Salford Crescent or Salford Central? I didn't want it to end. We pulled into Salford Crescent and I held my breath. The doors opened and still she sat there, tapping away with her fingers, our legs glued together. Yes! One more stop.

Ok, I thought, let's see how far this can go shall we? So, slowly, very very slowly, I began to relax my leg, letting the weight gradually fall towards her. The pressure increased until we were both resting completely against each other, our legs even started to sway a little as the train weaved along the track, but with the contact remaining firm and definite. 'Next stop Salford Central' and in a moment she was up and away. My eyes were glued to her as she left. I watched her walk past the window and away along the platform, but she never looked back.

The next day, I am sitting in my usual seat at the table, forward facing, book in hand and I'm trying to concentrate, trying to forget what happened the day before. But as we pull into Horwich Parkway, I can't help but search for her on the platform, my eyes darting left and right searching for her striking red coat. There she is! I quickly look back to my book, pretending not to have seen her as she boards, but I can't help but glance up as I sense her striding down the aisle towards me, her long coat parting with every step she takes, giving me a precious glimpse of her forbidden stockings. I assume they're stockings. I quickly look back to my book as she approaches and wait for her to pass me. But she stops. And she sits. And she's there, again.

I daren't look, I fix my eyes on the book, trying to read: *There are three empty saddles, but I see no Hobbits.* But I'm not taking it in, my mind is spinning in anticipation. I glance up for a millisecond and there she is, head back, eyes closed, pink headphones, smiling away to herself as we leave the station. Her fingers tap away to the beat as she shuffles slightly in her seat, getting comfortable for our journey. I wait, my leg waits, the hairs on my knee reaching out for her. I could edge towards her but it wouldn't be right, I have to wait. It happens so slowly, and for a minute or so I'm not even sure if we're touching or not, but then we turn a corner and she's there, her leg boldly swaying with mine, a forbidden tango under the melamine table. I can feel the nylon rubbing against my trousers, just millimetres of man-made fabric separating our lusting flesh. I turn page after page but I'm not reading a word, my mind is lost in what is possibly the most erotic moment of my life. The journey flies by in a blur and before I know it she's gone again, without a word or a smile.

Every day for two weeks this happened, and it was sheer perfection. No eye contact, no "hello", the perfect compromise. To all the world we were just two regular commuters, sticking to the code... perfect... until this morning.

8:09... I'm on my spot, ready, a minute early, waiting for the little three carriage train to arrive. But as I see it approach I start to panic. It's a replacement train, there's four, five, no six carriages, it's a monster! What do I do?! Where do I sit?! How will she find me?! I climb on board about half way down and quickly look both ways, empty seats everywhere, I hurry from carriage to carriage trying to work out where she'll get on, but we're moving already and soon we'll be at her stop. I have to be sitting down when we pull in. Eventually I reach the last carriage, I choose a table on our usual side and sit down just as we pull into Horwich Parkway. I'm so far back that I can't see her get on, all I can do is wait. I get out my book. The train leaves, still no sign of her. I look at the words but I can't focus. Shit, she'll think I'm avoiding her. She'll be sitting down already, probably on her own, or even worse with some stranger. Maybe there's still time, maybe I can find her. I close my book and begin to stand... / shit there she is, sweeping through the empty carriage towards me. I look down but it's too late, our eyes met: first rule broken.

I can feel my heart pounding as she slides into the seat. I fix my gaze on the trees flashing by and try to act like it hasn't happened, but it has happened, and everything's wrong. Instead of excitement it's... awkward, and we're alone! Our legs clumsily come together, it's horrible, I open my book and try to read, shit it's upside down, I look up to see if she's noticed, she's looking right at me, shit, bollocks, look out the window, focus, trees, power lines, sky, Dawn... Dawn... I look at her. She's smiling at me. She's giggling. 'My name's Dawn.'

Pause

My name's James.

Nice to meet you James.

And with that, she puts her hand on mine, leans across the table, and kisses me. It wasn't a snog, it wasn't a peck... it was a kiss. I've never been kissed like that before. One kiss and suddenly I'm picturing our lives together, our house, our children. James and Dawn. Not James and Nina. Nina... is my wife.

Oh God, what am I going to do?

This is where I get off.

SCENE 7: **Claire: PART 3**

What dae men really want in a woman? I mean I have the requisite 'parts'. I am still plumbed despite the equipment recently falling into disuse. This is a shite job but at least I have a one – I'm earnin'. I'm no' very good at it – I cannae remember the code fur cucumber. I aways ha' tae call Mary over. Mind, sometimes I dae it just to piss her off. She gets so easily radgey it's reyt funny. Brightens mah day no end. (*spies another customer*) Speaking of brightenin' mah day – here comes another twat, ooh actually he's quite fit!

(*flirty*) Hello! How are you? ...Good good... I see you've gone fae the three fae two offer – very wise, very wise! Ooh, and sausages! Yum yum! I like a bit of sausage mahself! (*no response*) Right £7.28 please. (*handed cash*) Thank you.

Pfff! I was trying my best moves on him, and he wasnae having any of it. He didnae laugh at mah jokes. Sense of humour. Maybe I'll havtae insist on that. (*getting up*) Mary! I'm going for a smoke!

(*whilst lighting a cigarette*) I do like a laugh... usually at other people. Like Alan the new shelf stacker – he's only got one arm! Och dinnae judge – y'thought the same as me. (*beat*) Right, plumbed, sense of humour, got a job: what more can a man want?

SCENE 8:   Colin: PART 2

Colin is at work, replying to an email.

...fucking massive bell-end! Yes, I noticed that you marked it as urgent, just like you do with every single email you send me, you tit! How is it even slightly urgent? Last week I spent three hours going through the whole report, replacing every occurrence of 'quick win' with 'tit wank'. So, unless everyone in the Strategic Co-Ordination Unit agrees that 'we need more tit wanks to satisfy stakeholders', I strongly suspect that, like everything else that goes on in this department, it's a complete waste of fucking time. For this reason, and also because it's five to five on a Friday, you jobs-worth twat, it can wait till Monday. Kind Regards, Colin.

He takes a deep meditative breath.

Surf the urge, Colin. Focus on the breath.

Select all and... delete.

Another deep calming breath. He starts to type again.

Hi Nina, apologies, I was unaware of the severity of the urgency, I will do all I can to get it done before close of play. Have a good weekend, Colin. Smiley Face. Send.

Beat

Four minutes to Five.

Beat

Fuck it, I'm going.

SCENE 9:   **Nina and James**

James is packing his bag. He hears the door open and close. He's surprised and stops packing, he hurriedly shoves the bag into a cupboard. There is also a supermarket carrier bag on the table.

Nina: (*off*) Hi. Are you there?

James: er...Yeh

Nina enters.

James: Hey. You're home early.

Nina: Don't sound too pleased about it.

Nina kisses James absently, by way of habit.

James: You ok? Good day?

Beat

Nina: er yeh... thanks. You?

James: Yeh, you know, same old, same old.

Nina: Did you go shopping?

James: er... Yeh.

Nina: Great, thanks. What did you get for dinner?

James apologetically indicates the bag on the table. Nina looks inside.

Nina: Seriously? Mince and potatoes? Inspiring stuff James! Did you even get any of the stuff on the list?

No response

James! Toilet roll? Bread? Cinnamon?!

James: Erm, no sorry...

Nina: Great! Thanks for that.

James: Sorry, I was distracted... and in a rush...

Nina: In a rush? What for? To get home to watch Top Gear repeats? Jesus!

James: Well... did you get the car tax sorted?

Beat

Nina: erm, no... sorry. I didn't have time.

James: C'mon Nina, what's the point in working in the public sector if you don't make use of your two hour lunches?

Nina: I do not have two hour lunches!

James: Well how long a lunch break did you have then?

Nina: Actually I didn't have a lunch break today. I had to... I had a last minute, urgent meeting. Coterminous target pathways...

James: (*mocks*) What? You've been rumbled?!

Nina: Don't!

James: What?

Nina: Make fun of my job. I've had a shit day as it is.

James: I was just joking. (*under his breath*) Fucking hell.

Nina collects a bottle of Chateauneuf du Pape and one glass.

James: err? What are you doing with that? We're saving that for a special occasion!

Nina ignores him and pours herself a glass.

Nina: Well, what can I make with these exotic, inspiring ingredients... mince and potatoes... or... shepherd's pie or... or... No that's it, options exhausted. Ooh and we better not make it too spicy as we've only got three sheets of toilet paper!

Nina throws a potato at him. Silence

Nina: Sorry. I'm being. Shit.

James: S'ok me too. And, er me too.

They laugh weakly.

James: C'mere. (*pulls her in for a hug*)

They hug for longer than usual. Each unsure what to do, but appreciating the comfort. James's phone rings, breaking the moment. Nina picks the phone out of his pocket and looks at the caller display.

Nina: Unknown.

James: (*shaken*) I best get this. It might be... work. (*he goes to leave the room*) Hello? James Reynolds speaking... (*as he leaves, a hint of disappointment in his voice*) Oh, hiya John...

Pause

She retrieves her own phone from her handbag. She rings a phone number from her contacts. Waits for an answer.

Nina: Hiya Sarah. How are you? ...Yeh not bad, just fancied a chat... (*trying to feign enthusiasm*) Oh has he? Erm... what did he say? Right... yeh great! He'll be reciting Shakespeare before you know it! No, hun, it's alright, no... no don't put him on... (*too late...*) Hello Oscar! How are you? Can you please put mummy back on? (*to herself*) No of course not. (*listens to babble for a bit, close to tears.*) Yes, very good Sarah... No I'm fine, just a bad day, I guess... Right ok, no go, it sounds like he needs you. Yeh... bye...

Nina stares at the wine. She takes a massive swig.

Shop announcement: over scene change

Mary: At our check-outs today, why not purchase one of our environmentally friendly carrier bags? Use me. Reuse me. Try not to lose me. Thank you.

SCENE 10:   Claire: PART 4

I confess! It's true I dunnae make jam and I cannae iron. I'm no' one of those homely wholesome women who provides a man wi' a ready-made substitute for his mother. Get to fuck! (*beat*) Mah mother doesnae think much a' mae. And she's supposed tae be biased... towards me right? Mah mother's ultimate smite: I dunnae feature much in her Christmas newsle'er. You can actually hear the disdain in her voice as she writes: 'Claire is livin' in England. She is currently working in retail whilst she contemplates her next career move'. Fuck off Ma – all I'm contempla'ing is how I'm gonna get some fuckin' cock! Gah, I know I'm a disappoin'ment to mah ma and I know she thinks I'm no' makin' the most of mahself.

But I tell ye what I have dun. Somethin' that *she*'s never had the fuckin' guts to dae.

I was able to admi' I wasnae happy. *I* was able tae stand up and say no more. No more Saturday afternoon beatings, whether Rangers won or lost. No more being told I'm a thick cunt. I'm no' a victim anymore. I'm Claire. And ye know what? I think I'm alright. I jus' need tae find a man who thinks so too.

(*to new customer – Dawn*) Hiya hen, ye want any help with y' packin'? Och I love y'coat! The red really brings oot the colour of yer eyes (*heartfelt response from Dawn, compliment about Claire's hair*) Aw! Thanks very much! (*Claire's phone starts to ring*) Och shite! That's ma phone! (*Dawn suggests Claire can answer it – she doesn't mind*) Och are ye sure?

(*Claire roots around in her pocket to answer the phone. During the phone call Claire continues to scan Dawn's items, take her money, give her receipt, waves goodbye etc*)

Hello? ...oh hiya! I didnae think ye'd have the balls tae ring me! Y've had ma number fae two weeks! ...ha ha, yep, seize the day! So... now that's y've seized it, what're gonna dae with it? ...meet up? Y'mean in the real world? Not just hiding behind a computa screen? ...yeh, no I do... Right... Yeh that soounds nice. I'll see ye in toon at 7 then?

(*to audience*) That was 'sexymister78'. We've bin chattin' online fae ages an' he seems pretty into mae... And ah I quite like him too. Right! Mary, I'm off!

Ah shite! I didnae tell him where we should meet... Och I'll ring him in a bit, dunnae want to seem too keen!

SCENE 11: Gareth

Gareth is sat at a table with a bowl of cereal and a glass of water. He is staring into space with a spoonful of cereal suspended in front of him. He finally snaps out of it.

> Fucking hell, what's wrong with me?

He drops the spoon into the bowl and takes a big gulp of water.

> Doesn't mean anything.

He stares at the glass of water.

> It was just a dream, just a vivid...scary...fucked up dream.

He lifts the spoon to his mouth.

> Well, not scary, scary now yeah.

He slams the spoon down.

> NO! Why the fuck is it scary? Nothing happened, nothing's changed, now fucking snap out of it!

He picks up the spoon and tries to eat the cereal, munching painfully, struggling to swallow. He finally manages to force it down but gags, almost being sick. He pushes the bowl away.

> Oh God, I feel sick.

He notices someone walking in, Gareth forces a smile.

Morning... Yeah good, yeah... oh, about 12ish, you? ...ah probably just missed you then...no, no didn't hear a thing, out like a light... no thanks, I'm fine with my water...

Sausages? ...oo, bit extravagant for a Tuesday, no thanks, I'd best stick to the cereal... oh, yeah, well it tastes a bit weird, I think the milk might be off... no not off, really don't know why I said that haha, I just feel a bit weird-tired-SICK! I didn't sleep too well to be honest... no, honestly it wasn't you ...just a weird dream, you know.

Really? Oh, what was yours about? ...No come on... haha why? Was I in it? ...ohhhh... shit... yeah well they're pretty freaky anyway aren't they, with their little arms and legs and massive heads and that... well no, but I mean if there were like, thousands of them, chanting and staring at you like that, I mean that would freak me out, but, no I love dwarves generally... people with dwarfism, yeah, sorry, I didn't know that one, it's a minefield these days innit? I only found out last year that half castes were called 'mixed race'... haha yeah right... oh right sorry... I just thought you, had a, nice tan... no not nice! I don't mean like 'attractive' or anything, god no! I just thought you were tanned, I mean I'm sure you are very attractive to some people, you're just not my type are you? Haha! You were in my dream and I kissed you! Oh Bollocks! Sorry.

He looks down at the table and goes back to eating his cereal. Very awkward silence.

> Look I'm really sorry about that... no, no it's not alright! I mean you've only just moved in and the last thing I wanted to do was make you feel uncomfortable... you're sure? ...Exactly! It's just a dream! That's what I've been sat here telling myself for the last four hours. I mean it was a dream and we were kissing, and naked and... yeah, probably best... you just cook your sausages and I'll, eat my cereal!

Another awkward silence, but not as long as before.

> By the way if you're ever short of cereal just help yourself to mine. This stuff was on offer, 3 for 2, only I'm not that keen on it to be honest, bit too nutty... well maybe you could pick the nuts out? ...well I'm just saying if you've got nothing in... right, no worries... I suppose what I'm trying to say is, what's mine is yours, share and share alike, as they say... except my bed of course! Ha! That's just a joke!

Silence.

> So what do you think the Dwar... fism people represented? ...hmmm, yeah, maybe, look I'm just going to have to tell you about my dream because it's really fucking my head up... well I'm just going to tell you anyway... right so I was kissing

you and we were naked and then... Why are you covering your ears – that is so childish!

He stands and starts to shout.

RIGHT, WELL, I'M KISSING YOU AND WE'RE NAKED AND I NOTICE THAT OUR COCKS ARE TOUCHING AND WE'RE BOTH REALLY HARD AND THEN I'M INSIDE YOU, BALLS DEEP AND THEN SOMEHOW, ONCE THE UNICORN HAS LEFT, YOU'RE INSIDE ME TOO, REACHING ROUND TO FONDLE MY MASSIVE BREASTS. AND THEN WE MORPH INTO THIS HUGE PULSATING BIRDS NEST OF COCKS AND ARSES AND KISSING AND TITS AND THEN I WAKE UP AND I'M CRYING AND I'VE MADE A RIGHT MESS.

He sits and starts to awkwardly move his spoon around the bowl.

Are you gay? ...no me neither...

Silence.

Your sausages need turning.

SCENE 12:   Cara

(*clutching Take a Break*)

What do I want? Well... I want to lose weight – obviously! That's why I've joined the gym - I'm trying to 'get in shape', well... *out* of shape I suppose – less like a Wagon Wheel more like a Twix.

I have been meaning to join the gym for ages but the final push to actually go was... (*pause*) not being able to reach round to wipe my own arse. I mean, you can only ask so much of your dad – he'll only do it when he's drunk and he's just joined AA, so... I did consider improvising with a sort-of flossing motion with some old towels. But then I thought I might as well put the money I would be spending on washing powder to gym membership. Do you know, they didn't have a box for that on the 'reason for joining form' so I just ticked 'other'. And so I joined the gym. 1 session, 450 pounds lighter. Shame it was sterling.

I didn't *want* to join the gym. I've tried everything going to avoid it. Weight Watchers, Slimming World, Lighter Life. "Find the new you", "Rediscover the old you". "Dear God: Anything but the current you". Shakes, bars, soups. RYVITA! Desperately trying to find... inventive ways of substituting cottage cheese into my favourite dishes – lasagne, curry, cheesecake... I even considered going for one of them gastric bands, cos they're supposed to work wonders aren't they? But apparently they mean you can't actually eat very much! So I don't see the point. I pride myself on getting value for money at the all you can eat – "the more you eat the more you save". That's what mum always says, well, said. She passed away last year – she slipped in the bathroom and hit her head, in the kitchen.

They've told me at the gym that technically I'm obese. But that's only cos I'm short for my weight. I mean, if I were seven foot two I'd be ideal. I've always *felt* taller than I am... And it says in here (*indicates Take a Break*) that 'the key to weight loss is a mind-set' so I'm half way there really.

Anyway... the gym is very nice. Jacuzzi, sauna, steam room. And... you know 'exercise machines'. They've all got a calorie burning calculator but I don't think they work. The other day, I'd done 4 minutes 34 on the stepper – non-stop – and it said I'd only burnt 23 calories. I mean, c'mon! 4 minutes 34? I reckon that's' equivalent to... a box of Jaffa Cakes. Ooh – and they're orange so they probably count as one of your five a day.

I'll be honest with you, I haven't actually, technically, been to the gym today. (*beat*) I have shown willing though. I mean I've put my sports bra on – and that's half the battle really intit? – having your breasts properly supported. I mean, I feel more athletic just wearing it.

I haven't always been fat. When I were 20 I were a size 12. I'm 28 now and I'm a size 20. And much as it is satisfying, maths-wise, to maintain a formula of: *age minus 8 = size*, I have accepted I should probably do something about it.

Otherwise by the time I'm 50 I'll have to buy clothes from Go Camping.

Anyway, my friends keep saying they like me as I am – I'm 'jolly'. My size is part of what makes me, me. But you know what? I *hate* being fat. I want to be able to walk up the stairs without panting, I want to be able to wear a skirt without getting chubb rub and ending up walking like John Wayne to avoid further chafing! I want someone to tell me I'm beautiful and I want to be able to believe it.

Oh sorry, what do I want? Oh I see what you mean... I'll have a Big Mac meal please... Diet coke.

SCENE 13: Colin and Claire

Claire's living room. There are clothes strewn on the sofa.

Claire enters, closely followed by Colin. Claire takes her shoes off.

Claire: Ok, well this is me, oh shite, sorry aboot th'mess.

Colin: Shoes off is it? (*taking off his shoes*)

Claire: (*gathering up the clothes and taking them into the other room*) I'm no' in the habit of bringin' men back on the first date

Colin playfully grabs her from behind and kisses her neck.

Claire: ...but you sir are very persuasive. And I couldnae resist the urge y'kno?

Colin: Ohhhh yes I get you.

They kiss.

Colin pulls away, teasing.

Colin: What do you have to do to get a drink round here then?

Claire: Y' cheeky shite. I didnae think it was my – well stocked drinks cabinet that had lured you.

Colin:	Oh believe me it wasn't. (*He pulls her back close and kisses her again*) But I could really murder a bourbon.
Claire:	Are y'takin' the piss? Y'll have a single malt or y'getting nowhere near my bedroom.
Colin:	(*making fun of her accent*) You really are a feisty wee betch. Malt it is then.
Claire:	Good lad. (*as she exits to the kitchen*) Ice?
Colin:	Nah, save that for the bedroom!
Claire:	(*off*) Ha! Ye'll dae fa me!

Colin sits on the sofa but realises he's sat on something. He pulls an iron out from under the cushion. He holds it in front of him, gazing at it. He glances in the direction that Claire exited and then looks back at the iron. Claire enters with the drinks.

Claire:	Christ! What are y'doin' with that?
Colin:	(*snapping out of his trance*) It was... on the sofa.
Claire:	Right, but what are y'doin' with it?
Colin:	I just... er... sorry!

They stand in silence. Colin is still holding the iron.

Claire:	Can ye *just* put it doon, pleaze.

Colin:	Yeh! Sorry. Don't look so worried - it's not like I was going to hit you with it or anything! (*laughs awkwardly*)
Claire:	(*firmly*) Colin... please, dunnae joke aboot that!
Colin:	Ok, sorry!
Claire:	No it's fine.

Silence

Claire:	Anyway, cheers!

They clink glasses. Claire moves in for a kiss. They kiss and then.

Colin:	Are you not gonna put that away?
Claire:	What?
Colin:	The iron.
Claire:	Oh. Right, if it's botherin' *you*. I mean, it's not botherin' me... honest!

She puts her drink down, picks up the iron and exits to the kitchen.

Colin:	Sorry, I'm just a bit funny with... clutter.

Claire re-enters.

Claire: No it's fine, dunnae want it distracting ye do we? (*beat*) Your place is all minimalist I bet.

Colin: Tidy house, tidy mind.

Claire: Well, if you wake before me, feel free to throw the duster aroond a bit, I willnae be offended.

Colin: Oh, so I am staying the night?

Claire looks Colin in the eyes.

Claire: Might as well eh?

Claire kisses him again. Colin doesn't reciprocate.

Claire: OK, what's wrong?

Colin: Your keys.

Claire: What / aboot them?

Colin: You locked the door when we came in.

Claire: So?

Colin: It's just that you… should always leave your keys in the door, just in case.

Claire: In case of what?

Colin: Well, in case you need to get out in a hurry. For whatever reason.

Claire: (*sarcastically*) Ye mean in case there's a fire?

Colin: Yeah exactly! A fire. There'd be smoke everywhere / so you don't want to be rooting through your bag for your keys.

Claire: Look I'd rather ye just told me if you're plannin' on doing a runner in the mornin'.

Colin: What?! No, no that's not what I meant!

Claire: It's what it soounds like / from where I'm standin'.

Colin: I promise, it's not like that.

Claire: Go on then: explain! I'm all ears.

Colin: Ok... (*beat*) ...could you just get your keys first though?

Claire: Oh fur fuck's sake, fine!

Claire grabs her bag, fishes out her keys and chucks them on the table.

Colin: Ok. Right. Well I didn't want to tell you this online because... erm... / well it's difficult to explain really.

Claire: Jeezo Col, just say it!

Colin: I really like you, Claire...

Claire: (*interrupting*) But you're married?

Colin: What? NO! No, it's not that!

Claire: Well, what is it then?

Colin: I think you're the most amazing girl I've ever met.

Claire: (*sarcastically*) Yeh right! We only met five hours ago!

Colin: But we've chatted online so much, I know you. And you are. You are amazing!

Claire: Pfff!

Colin: I mean it! You're funny, clever, / sexy

Claire: Ha! I'm no' clever... sexy maybe, but not clever.

Colin: Well, you know loads of long words.

Claire: Knowin' long words / dusnae make me clever.

Colin: And you're so... open. You think it, and you say it. You're just... you. I love that.

Claire: (*hesitant*) What y'see is what y'get, I suppose.

Beat

Claire: Thank you.

Colin: You're welcome.

Claire: But…?

Colin: I'm sorry.

Claire: Why?

Colin: I want to be like that… I really want this to be out of my head… but I don't know / how to explain it.

Claire: Whatever's in yer head just… say it.

Colin takes a deep breath and composes himself. He stands, and very determinedly picks up the keys and puts them firmly in Claire's hand.

Colin: Ok. I don't know… but here goes… Ok. So you're sat in the theatre right. You're sat there watching a play and it's… ok, I mean it's not amazing, but it's, you know, keeping your attention…

Music up, lights fade out

END